The*Vermeer*Interviews

Conversations with Seven Works of Art

as imagined by **BOB** *RACZKA*

M Millbrook Press/Minneapolis

To Carol, *thanks for helping me bring this book to life*

Text copyright © 2009 by Bob Raczka

Millbrook Press
A division of Lerner Publishing Group, Inc.
241 First Avenue North
Minneapolis, MN 55401 U.S.A.

Website address: www.lernerbooks.com

Library of Congress Cataloging-in-Publication Data

Raczka, Bob.
    The Vermeer interviews : conversations with seven works of art / by Bob Raczka.
       p.   cm.
    Includes bibliographical references.
    ISBN: 978–0–8225–9402–4 (lib. bdg. : alk. paper)
    1. Vermeer, Johannes, 1632–1675—Juvenile literature. I. Vermeer, Johannes, 1632–1675. II. Title.
    ND653.V5R34 2009
    759.9492—dc22   2008024969

Manufactured in the United States of America
1 2 3 4 5 6 – DP – 14 13 12 11 10 09

Cover art courtesy of: Kunsthistoriches Museum (KHM), Wien.

Interior art courtesy of: © iStockphoto.com/Bill Noll, backgrounds on pp. 1, 2, 3, 5, 6, 7, 9, 10, 11, 13, 14, 15, 17, 18, 19, 21, 22, 23, 25, 26, 27, 29, 30, 31, 32; © Laura Westlund/Independent Picture Service, p. 3 (top); © The Bridgeman Art Library/Getty Images, p. 3 (bottom); © iStockphoto.com/Patricia Hofmeester, backgrounds on pp. 4, 8, 12, 16, 20, 24, 28; Rijksmuseum, Amsterdam, pp. 4, 16, 22; Delft Tiles, c.1750–1800 (earthenware), Dutch School, (18th century) / © Collection of the New-York Historical Society, USA / The Bridgeman Art Library International, pp. 5 (top), 6, 7; Royal Cabinet of Paintings, Mauritshuis, The Hague, p. 5 (bottom); © Städel Museum //ARTOTHEK, p. 8; © The New York Public Library/Art Resource, NY, p. 9; © National Maritime Museum, Greenwich, London, pp. 10, 11; Kunsthistoriches Museum (KHM), Wien, p. 12; © Vanni/Art Resource, NY, p. 13; National Archives (RG 111-SC-204516), p. 14; © akg-images/Universiteits Bibliotheek, p. 17; Courtesy of the Delft Municipal Archives, p. 19; The Metropolitan Museum of Art, Marquand Collection, Gift of Henry G. Marquand, 1889 (89.15.21) Image © The Metropolitan Museum of Art, p. 20; © Art Resource, NY, p. 21; Willem Janszoon Blaeu, Map of Delft, 1648, p. 23; © Bildarchiv Preussischer Kulturbesitz/Art Resource, NY, p. 24; © pulp/Photodisc/Getty Images, pp. 25, 26 (bottom), 27; The Guitar Player, c.1672 (oil on canvas), Vermeer, Jan (1632–75) / The Iveagh Bequest, Kenwood House, London, UK / The Bridgeman Art Library International, p. 26 (top); The Royal Collection © 2008 Her Majesty Queen Elizabeth II, p. 28; Cantus p.223, Latin mass with illuminated letter A / British Library, London, UK, © DACS / © British Library Board. All Rights Reserved / The Bridgeman Art Library International, pp. 29, 31; © Lebrecht Music & Arts/The Image Works, p. 30.

Introduction

Johannes (or Jan) Vermeer is one of the most popular painters in the history of art. Yet we know very little about him.

Jan Vermeer lived in Delft. This map shows modern country names and borders.

Written records of Vermeer's life and his paintings are scarce. We know he was born in 1632, died in 1675, and lived in Delft, a city in modern-day Netherlands. But we don't have any of Vermeer's early sketches or drawings. We don't have any letters he may have written. We don't even know who his teachers were.

Most of what we know about Vermeer, we have learned by studying his paintings. However, Vermeer made very few paintings during his lifetime. And not all of them have survived to this day. Some art scholars say just thirty-four remain. Others say as many as thirty-six.

When I look at a Vermeer painting, I often feel as though I'm interrupting someone in a personal moment. Somehow, this feeling makes the people in his paintings seem more real. Many of Vermeer's paintings look like photographs, which adds to their realness.

Several art historians believe Vermeer used an early form of the camera to compose his paintings. Called a *camera obscura,* this was a large wooden box with a lens at one end. Instead of taking pictures like a modern camera, it projected the scene the artist wanted to paint onto the back wall of the box. There the painter could study the image, or even trace it, to make paintings more true to life.

But no matter what techniques Vermeer used to bring his paintings to life, I wanted to know more about them. So I decided to interview a few of my favorites. As you are about to see, these paintings are as alive today as they were more than three hundred years ago when Vermeer created them.

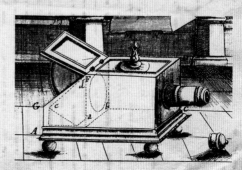

camera obscura

The Milkmaid *(ca. 1658–1660), Rijksmuseum, Amsterdam*

An Everyday *Beauty*

A Conversation with The Milkmaid

BOB: You have always been one of Vermeer's most popular paintings. Does this surprise you?

MAID: You mean because I'm just a maid?

BOB: Well, I wouldn't put it quite that way.

MAID: It's okay. I know I'm not as pretty or mysterious as the *Girl with a Pearl Earring*. But I don't measure myself against other paintings.

BOB: You are referring of course to one of Vermeer's other portraits, called *Girl with a Pearl Earring*. She certainly has been popular lately, with both a book and movie being made about her. Do you hope to be the subject of a book or a movie someday?

MAID: Heavens no. She's a lovely girl, and I'm happy for her, but we're two completely different paintings.

BOB: You said earlier, "I'm just a maid," but there is something beautiful and even heroic about you.

MAID: Thank you for saying so. Master Vermeer was very good at capturing the beauty of everyday life. I'm just a housemaid pouring milk, but somehow he made me more than that. He used many visual tricks.

BOB: Like what?

MAID: Oh, like playing with light and dark. Look at **my right hand**, the one holding the handle of the pitcher. Do you see how the light coming through the window makes it bright?

Girl with a Pearl Earring
(ca. 1665–1666)

BOB: Yes, I can see that.

MAID: However, the **wall behind my hand** is dark, because it's in shadow. So my right hand stands out. This draws your eyes to the only action in the painting, which is my pouring the milk.

BOB: You're right, it does.

MAID: Now if you look at the **left side of my body**, the part farthest from the window, you'll see that it's in shadow. But the wall behind that part of me is bright. So the entire left side of my body appears to come forward, making me look more three-dimensional. Master Vermeer understood that putting bright areas next to dark areas creates this effect. I believe he called it *contrast*.

BOB: That's amazing.

MAID: That's why Vermeer is sometimes called the painter of light.

BOB: What other visual tricks did he use?

MAID: Look at the **blue cloth** flowing off the edge of the table. Do you see how it's directly under the milk flowing out of the pitcher?

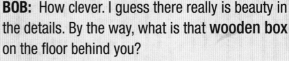

BOB: Now that you've pointed it out, I do.

MAID: That is no accident. Master Vermeer did that so the flowing movement would continue right off the canvas.

BOB: How clever. I guess there really is beauty in the details. By the way, what is that **wooden box** on the floor behind you?

MAID: That is a foot warmer. Filled with hot coals, it comes in quite handy during our cold Dutch winters. By the way, do you see the **blue and gray tiles** behind the foot warmer? Those were made here in Delft. In addition to being decorative, they protect the plaster walls from sweeping and mopping.

BOB: Do you have a favorite detail in this painting?

MAID: Well, since you ask, I do love the **broken windowpane**.

BOB: Wow. I've seen this painting dozens of times and never noticed that before.

MAID: That's what I love about it—the fact that most people don't see it. It's one of those little things that makes me feel at home.

BOB: You do look at home, so satisfied and focused on your work. I can almost hear you humming a tune to yourself. Do you ever hum?

MAID: Well, let's just say I haven't had many other ways to pass the time over the last three hundred years!

BOB: I read somewhere that Vermeer based your pose on an earlier Italian painting of a queen.

MAID: Yes, *Queen Artemisia* (art-uh-MIZ-ee-uh) by Domenico Fiasella (do-MEN-ee-koh fee-ah-ZELL-uh).

BOB: Do you ever wish you were a queen instead of a maid?

MAID: Never. I'm very happy with who I am.

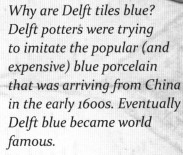

Why are Delft tiles blue? Delft potters were trying to imitate the popular (and expensive) blue porcelain that was arriving from China in the early 1600s. Eventually Delft blue became world famous.

The Geographer *(ca. 1668–1669), Städelsches Kunstinstitut, Frankfurt am Main*

A Bit of *Wanderlust*

A Conversation with The Geographer

BOB: Most of Vermeer's paintings show women who are busy with some sort of quiet activity. But two of his paintings are of men who are scientists. Why do you suppose he painted you, a geographer?

GEOG: I believe it had to do with the advances being made in geography at the time. European explorers and traders were discovering new worlds. Mapmaking techniques were improving. In fact, the Netherlands had become a center for mapmaking.

BOB: Were the maps in this painting made in the Netherlands?

GEOG: Most definitely. Master Vermeer painted his maps so accurately that historians can identify their publishers. For example, the **map on the wall** behind me is a sea chart published by Willem Janszoon Blaeu (VILL-em YAHN-tsen BLAU). The **globe** above my head was published by Hendrick Hondius (HEN-drick HAHN-dee-uhs). Both were based in Amsterdam, a city not far from Delft.

BOB: One of my favorite things about this painting is the **thoughtful expression** on your face. I can't help but wonder what you're thinking about.

GEOG: Yes, I do have a lot on my mind.

BOB: Some people think you are experiencing a moment of inspiration. But to me, it looks like you're suffering from a bit of wanderlust. The way you look up toward the outside world, I imagine that you're thinking about sailing to some of the far-off places on your maps.

World map by Willem Janszoon Blaeu (ca. 1635)

GEOG: That's interesting, because in Master Vermeer's original composition, I was actually looking down at my charts.

BOB: Really? So he painted over this original pose?

GEOG: Yes. Just to the left of my face you can see a **hazy, dark outline.** It matches the shape of my forehead, only it's tilted at a downward angle.

BOB: I see it.

GEOG: If Master Vermeer had left me looking down, instead of up, you might not have seen that wanderlust.

BOB: What a difference a single change can make. Did Vermeer make any other changes in this painting?

GEOG: On the little table in the lower right-hand corner, you can see the **ghost image** of a sheet of paper. If I remember correctly, Master Vermeer painted over the paper to make that corner darker. He was always balancing the light and dark areas in his paintings.

BOB: Fascinating. I've noticed that several of Vermeer's paintings feature **Oriental rugs,** like the one draped over your table. Is there a reason for this?

GEOG: As I said earlier, it was an age of exploration. By this time, the Dutch had established a shipping route to China and Japan—the globe behind me is actually turned to show this route. As a result, rugs and other goods from throughout Asia had become popular in the Netherlands. The **Japanese robe** I am wearing is another example.

BOB: What is the **tool** you're holding? It looks like a compass.

GEOG: It is a set of dividers. I use it to measure distances on charts and maps. You may also notice the **cross-staff** hanging between the windows. It is used to figure out the location of a ship at sea by measuring the distance between the North Star and the horizon.

Globe by Jodocus Hondius Jr., older brother of Hendrick Hondius (1613)

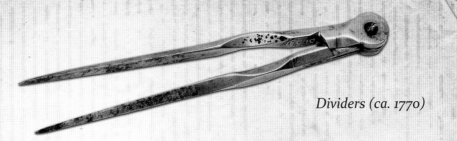

Dividers (ca. 1770)

BOB: Speaking of the stars, you look an awful lot like *The Astronomer*, Vermeer's other painting of a scientist.

GEOG: Very observant. Yes, Master Vermeer used the same model to paint us both.

BOB: Many art historians think the model for both you and *The Astronomer* was Antoni van Leeuwenhoek (AHN-ton-ee vahn LAY-ven-hook), the famous Delft scientist.

GEOG: I have heard that theory.

BOB: Wasn't he born in Delft in 1632, just like Vermeer?

GEOG: Yes, I believe he was.

BOB: I seem to remember that he was famous for improving the microscope and discovering many microscopic life-forms. But wasn't van Leeuwenhoek also skilled in navigation, astronomy, mathematics, and natural science?

GEOG: He was indeed.

BOB: Also, he would have been about thirty-six years old at the time you were painted—the same age you appear to be. Not to mention that when Vermeer died, van Leeuwenhoek was the one who carried out the instructions in his will. Based on all this, I have to believe that you are Antoni van Leeuwenhoek.

GEOG: As a man of science, I must admit your evidence is compelling.

The Artist in His Studio *(ca. 1665–1666), Kunsthistorisches Museum, Vienna*

The *Riddle* of the Sphinx

A Conversation with The Artist in His Studio

BOB: I'll get right to the point. None of Vermeer's known paintings are self-portraits. Yet because you are an artist, many people assume that you are Jan Vermeer (YAHN vir-MEER). Are you?

ARTIST: What do you think?

BOB: I like to think so. But I also think it's funny that, if you are Jan Vermeer, your only self-portrait is one that doesn't show your face.

ARTIST: Historians don't call Master Vermeer the Sphinx of Delft (SFINKS of DELFT) for nothing.

BOB: The Sphinx of Delft?

ARTIST: In Greek mythology, the Sphinx was a winged creature with a lion's body and a woman's head. It strangled anyone who couldn't answer its riddle. Later, the word *sphinx* came to mean any person who is difficult to know. Now, I'm fairly certain that Jan Vermeer never strangled anyone, but I have to agree that he is difficult to know.

BOB: So are you Jan Vermeer or not?

ARTIST: Let's just say that I knew him very well.

BOB: That's the kind of puzzling answer I'd expect from a sphinx. If you don't mind, I'd like to ask your lovely model a few questions. It looks like you're wearing a costume of some sort. Who are you pretending to be?

Greek sculpture of a Sphinx
(ca. 600–480 B.C.)

MODEL: Well, the horn I hold represents fame. The book in my hand is the works of Thucydides (thoo-SID-uh-deez), a classical Greek historian. And on my head are the laurels of victory. These are all symbols of Clio (KLAH-yoh), the Muse of History.

BOB: What exactly is a Muse?

MODEL: Like the Sphinx, the Muses come from Greek mythology. They were the nine daughters of Zeus, the king of the Greek gods. The ancient Greeks believed that the Muses watched over the arts and sciences, providing inspiration to people who worked in those fields.

BOB: So why is the artist painting you as the Muse of History?

MODEL: Because at this time, Dutch history was being made. The southern half of the Netherlands had recently won its independence from the Hapsburg (HAPS-burg) Empire, which ruled over much of Europe. It became a democracy known as the United Provinces. This new country was starting with a clean canvas, so to speak, just like the artist.

BOB: And by painting you, the artist is also "making history"?

MODEL: Precisely.

BOB: Speaking of history, I understand that you two had quite a scare during World War II.

ARTIST: Yes we did. In 1940 the German Nazi leader Adolf Hitler bought our painting. We ended up being stored in a salt mine outside of Salzburg, Austria, for five years, along with many other famous paintings. Many great pieces of art were destroyed during the war, but thankfully we survived.

General Dwight D. Eisenhower and other U.S. Army officials gather in a salt mine to examine art the Nazis stole (or forced owners to sell at low prices) during World War II. (April 12, 1945)

BOB: You certainly have lived through a lot. You know, I love the fact that there is an **empty chair** in the lower left-hand corner of this painting. It's as if Vermeer is inviting me to sit down and watch him— or should I say you—paint.

ARTIST: Master Vermeer would be happy to hear you say that. Yes, the empty chair is one of the ways that he invites you into this painting. The **hanging curtain** is another.

BOB: You're right, the curtain makes me want to reach out and pull it aside to see what's behind it.

ARTIST: You see? It works. Both the curtain and the chair are examples of a painter's trick called *repoussoir* (RAY-poo-swa), which creates an illusion of depth and draws you into the scene.

BOB: Incredible. I'd like to ask Clio just one more question. As the artist's model, you must know whether or not he is Jan Vermeer.

MODEL: I do.

BOB: Well?

MODEL: Some things are better left a mystery, don't you think?

BOB: Great, a Muse who thinks she's a sphinx. I guess I'll just have to content myself with pulling up the empty chair and watching you two work. Do you mind?

MODEL: Not at all.

ARTIST: Be our guest.

Woman in Blue Reading a Letter *(ca. 1662–1663), Rijksmuseum, Amsterdam*

How to *Read* a Painting

A Conversation with the Woman in Blue Reading a Letter

BOB: I was talking to *The Milkmaid* recently—do you know her?

WOMAN: Oh yes, our paintings both hang in the same museum in Amsterdam.

BOB: She was telling me that Vermeer used many visual tricks to make her look heroic. How did he make you look so quiet and still?

WOMAN: Where should I begin? The most obvious thing Master Vermeer did was to shape me like a **triangle**, wider at the bottom than at the top. This helps hold me in place. He also anchored me in the center of the painting.

BOB: Such simple devices, yet both are very effective.

WOMAN: Yes, and look at my hands. The **black bar** at the bottom of the **hanging map** seems to pin them in place, preventing them from moving.

BOB: Very clever. What about Vermeer's colors? Do they affect your mood?

WOMAN: Tremendously. The **blues and browns** Master Vermeer used to paint me are calming, peaceful colors. Imagine how different the mood of this painting would be if I were dressed in red.

BOB: I hate to be nosy, but I'm dying to know. Who sent you that letter?

WOMAN: I could just tell you, but what fun would that be? You can probably figure it out for yourself just by reading my painting.

Letter written in Dutch (1725)

BOB: How do you read a painting?

WOMAN: It's like being a—what would you call it?—a detective. You have to study all the visual clues in the painting to figure out what story the artist is telling.

BOB: Could you give me an example?

WOMAN: Of course. Try to read my body language first. Do you see how **my neck** is bent forward, how **my lips** are parted, and how I hold the letter with **both hands**, with my arms drawn in? What do you make of these clues?

BOB: That you've been eagerly waiting for this letter? That the information in it is important to you?

WOMAN: Those are both reasonable conclusions. What about the room around me? Does the **chair** in the foreground suggest anything? Or the **map** behind my head?

BOB: I'm not sure what you mean.

WOMAN: Well, I am alone. The chair is empty. And the map shows places that are quite far away.

BOB: I see. So the empty chair might suggest that the person who wrote the letter is missing from this room, and the map might suggest that this person is writing from far away?

WOMAN: Again, those guesses make sense based on the clues Master Vermeer has given you.

BOB: From the way **your clothes** fit, you look like you might be pregnant. Would that be a clue?

WOMAN: Now you're getting the idea. Many people agree that I look like I am with child.

BOB: I remember reading that Vermeer and his wife, Catharina (cat-uh-REE-nuh), had eleven children. With her being pregnant so often and with Vermeer needing a pregnant model—what I'm getting at is, are you Catharina?

The marriage record of Jan Vermeer and Catharina Bolnes (1653)

WOMAN: Many art scholars have wondered the same thing. For now, let's just say that I am with child and I've received a letter from someone far away, a letter that I've been waiting for. Whom do you think it is from?

BOB: It's seems so obvious now—your husband.

WOMAN: But you had to gather the clues before you could say so. And remember, this doesn't mean that other people won't read my painting differently.

BOB: How could someone possibly read this painting differently?

WOMAN: You think I look like I am with child. But some people think that the way my clothes fit, flaring out around my middle, was just part of the fashion of the time.

BOB: If that's the case, then the writer of the letter doesn't seem so obvious. And maybe you are not Vermeer's wife.

WOMAN: As I said, those were reasonable conclusions you made, based on how you read my painting. Others may not see me that way.

BOB: Is there a right way to read your painting?

WOMAN: Only Master Vermeer knows for sure. And he never told me.

Young Woman with a Water Pitcher *(ca. 1662),*
Metropolitan Museum of Art, New York

Reflections and Rectangles

A Conversation with the Young Woman with a Water Pitcher

BOB: You are wearing what looks like a **wide, white collar**. What is it?

WOMAN: It is called a *night rail,* a nightshirt for the shoulders. Dutch women wore these to bed and in the morning when getting dressed. As you can see, I am preparing to wash my face in the basin. The night rail helps protect my dress from splashing water.

BOB: Like most people who look at this painting, I would love to know why you are opening the window. You could just be letting in some fresh air, but I get the feeling that some sort of noise outside has interrupted you. Other people think that you're going to water the flowers in a window box.

From the 1500s to the 1800s, many Europeans avoided washing their full bodies, believing it could lead to sickness. But they did wash their faces and hands with basins and pitchers such as this set.

WOMAN: I love that idea!

BOB: Then there is that **blue dress** lying over the chair beside you and the **string of pearls** hanging from the **box** on the table. One art historian has suggested that by opening the window, you are looking forward to escaping the boredom of your daily life and dressing up for an evening out. Could you shed some light on all of this?

WOMAN: Isn't it remarkable how much of a story someone can create from just a few simple details? Of course, in the end, it doesn't really matter why I'm opening the window. What matters is that you are asking the question. It means that Master Vermeer has succeeded in making you curious, and he would be tickled to know it.

BOB: If he would be tickled by that, he would probably laugh out loud over this: I actually have this idea in my head that your view from the window is the same view shown in Vermeer's landscape painting *The Little Street*.

The Little Street *(ca. 1658)*

> **WOMAN:** I won't give away any secrets, but that's not as unlikely as you may think.

BOB: I love how Vermeer painted the reflections of the **blue sky** and **white clouds** in the **window**. It looks like a nice day in your painting.

> **WOMAN:** Any day you can spend being painted by a man called the painter of light is a nice day! But seriously, Master Vermeer never missed an opportunity to show off his skill at painting light. If you like how he handled the sky and clouds in the window, take a look at the reflection of the **Oriental rug** on the bottom of the **washbasin**.

BOB: I was just admiring that. You know, every time I look at one of Vermeer's paintings, I see something new. For instance, I notice the way he balanced **your hand** on the window by placing **your other hand** on the water pitcher.

> **WOMAN:** Yes, and you've only scratched the surface. You wouldn't believe how hard Master Vermeer worked to balance the composition of this painting.

BOB: Try me.

> **WOMAN:** Well, he started with rectangles. The **window**, the **table**, and the **map** are all rectangles, all similar in size. These three rectangles form a triangle within the painting, with me at the center. Did you notice how easily your eyes move from the window to the table to the map?

BOB: Now that you mention it, I do.

WOMAN: Now look at the **white spaces** between the window, the table, and the map. They're roughly rectangular as well. They form their own triangle that interlocks with the first. So everything is in balance.

BOB: How in the world did Vermeer think of all this?

WOMAN: Oh, there's more. Do you see how the window is blue, the table is red, and the map is yellow?

BOB: Let me guess—so the three primary colors are all represented equally.

WOMAN: Correct. And that's not all. Because my gaze pulls your eyes to the left, in the direction of the window, Master Vermeer put **more objects** on the right side of the painting to pull your eyes back.

BOB: I never realized how much thought and planning Vermeer put into his paintings.

WOMAN: That he did. Even so, Master Vermeer was not above trial and error. For example, there's a **slightly darker area** on the wall behind my head. He originally painted the map there, then changed his mind. And under my right arm, just to the right of the window, you can almost make out the **shape of a lion's head**. This was the carved part of a chair that he painted over.

BOB: I guess he was human after all. Still, you must feel lucky to have been painted by such an artistic genius.

WOMAN: Who wouldn't? People have been admiring me for centuries. A person doesn't get much luckier than that.

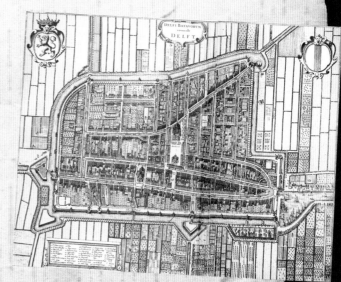

Map of Delft by Willem Janszoon Blaeu (1648)

Woman with a Pearl Necklace *(ca. 1664)*,
Gemäeldegalerie, Staatliche Museen zu Berlin

Mirror, *Mirror*

A Conversation with the Woman with a Pearl Necklace

BOB: You have been looking at yourself in the mirror for more than three hundred years now. Do you like what you see?

WOMAN: Well, I don't want to sound vain, but I have aged pretty well, don't you think? The truth is I feel very fortunate. Not many people get the chance to be around for as long as I have or to be painted by an artist as talented as Master Vermeer.

BOB: Many of Vermeer's paintings show women in private moments. But yours is the one that makes me feel the most like I'm invading someone's privacy, even more so than *Woman in Blue Reading a Letter*. I actually feel a little uncomfortable watching you. Does it seem strange to have people looking at you while you look at yourself?

WOMAN: You get used to it. We all like to watch other people when they think they're alone. We all eavesdrop now and then. Master Vermeer understood that allowing you to invade my privacy would draw you into the painting. And it worked. In the end, I'd much rather have people looking at me than not looking at me.

BOB: There is a **faint line** between you and the right edge of the canvas and another one along the top of the painting. Are they signs of damage?

WOMAN: After Master Vermeer finished this painting, he decided a smaller composition looked better. Those lines show where he originally framed it. Over the years, restorers reframed it to include what he left out.

BOB: I've noticed that your fur-lined **yellow jacket** is the same yellow jacket worn by the women in five other Vermeer paintings: *Woman with a Lute*, *A Lady Writing a Letter*, *Mistress and Maid*, *The Love Letter*, and *The Guitar Player*. Does this bother you?

The Guitar Player *(ca. 1672)*

WOMAN: I suppose it should. But no, it doesn't bother me. The jacket is so beautiful, you can see why Master Vermeer wanted to paint it again and again. I feel honored to be wearing something that was such a favorite of his.

BOB: Was yellow one of his favorite colors?

WOMAN: It certainly was. Just look at how much yellow is in this painting alone: the **curtain**, my **jacket**, my **blond hair**—even the **light in the room** has a yellow tint to it.

BOB: As with most Vermeer paintings, there seems to be an underlying story here. You are wearing a fancy jacket with a **red bow** in your hair. You have **pearls** hanging from your ears and a **string of pearls** around your neck. Then there is that mysterious **piece of paper** on the chair next to your dressing table. Are you getting ready to meet someone?

WOMAN: I know what you're thinking. You're thinking that because I'm making a fuss over how I look, the piece of paper must be a note from my secret admirer telling me when to meet him.

BOB: I take it other people have jumped to this conclusion.

WOMAN: It's human nature. You want to know why I'm getting dressed up, so you make up a story based on what you see in the painting. By including mysterious details, like the note on the chair, Master Vermeer encouraged viewers to "fill in the blanks." I think it's one of the reasons people enjoy his paintings so much.

BOB: In other words, as far as Vermeer is concerned, it's not important for me to know what the story behind the painting is. What's important is that I think there is one.

WOMAN: I couldn't have said it better myself.

BOB: I was recently reading something by an art critic who said that the real subject of this painting is not you but the **blank space** between you and the mirror. What do you think he meant by that?

WOMAN: I never thought about it that way, but I think I know what that person means. The blank wall allows my gaze to travel to and from the mirror uninterrupted, which creates a long moment of tension as I look at myself. Master Vermeer also made the **wall** brighter closer to the mirror, which makes my reflection look as if it is glowing.

BOB: I also read that Vermeer had originally sketched a map on that wall and then decided against it.

WOMAN: Yes, that's true, and you can see why. The map would have taken your attention away from my gaze and broken the tension.

BOB: So sometimes, knowing what to leave out of a painting is just as important as what to put in.

WOMAN: It sounds so simple, doesn't it? That's what Master Vermeer did best—he made the complicated look simple.

The Music Lesson *(ca. 1662–1665), The Royal Collection, London*

Two *Love* Stories

A Conversation with the Couple in The Music Lesson

BOB: The title of your painting is *The Music Lesson*. What kind of instrument is the young lady playing?

STUDENT: I am playing a virginal, which is a type of harpsichord.

TUTOR: If I may be more specific, a harpsichord is a stringed instrument played with keys. When the keys are pressed, a mechanism inside plucks the strings, similar to the way a harp player plucks a harp's strings. Most harpsichords are triangular in shape, but the virginal is box-shaped.

BOB: It's very decorative. As a music instructor, do you have any idea how much an instrument like this might cost?

TUTOR: This one was quite expensive. It was made by the world-famous Ruckers family in Antwerp, Belgium. In 1660 it cost in the neighborhood of 300 guilders.

BOB: Wow. In U.S. dollars, that's about $5,800. Obviously this is a wealthy household. There's an **inscription** on the lid of the instrument that looks like it's written in Latin. Can you tell me what it says?

STUDENT: *"Musica letitae comes medicina dolorum."* (MOO-see-kuh leh-TEE-tay KOH-mes meh-dee-CHEE-nuh doh-LOH-room.) Translated from Latin, it means, "Music is the companion of joy, the medicine for sorrow."

BOB: What a beautiful thought. So in this painting, is your music the companion of joy or the medicine for sorrow?

STUDENT: What do you mean?

BOB: Well, I get the impression that you two have feelings for each other beyond your relationship as student and tutor. Vermeer painted you so close together. And then there's the way **your tutor** looks at you.

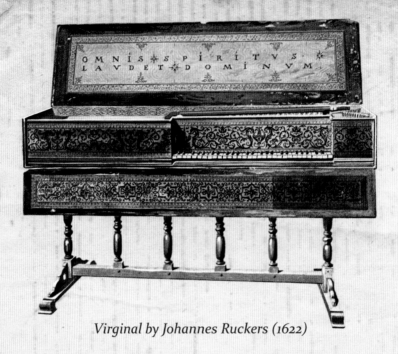

Virginal by Johannes Ruckers (1622)

STUDENT: I'm not sure I feel comfortable talking about this.

BOB: Forgive me. But you're part of such an intriguing painting. And you must know that people enjoy a good love story.

TUTOR: If I may, I'd like to answer your question. For me, this is a scene of both joy and sorrow. I am joyful to be in the same room with this lovely and talented young lady. But I'm sorrowful that I will never be any closer to her, even just to hold her hand. Her music makes me feel both glad and sad.

STUDENT: Now that he has spoken, I can't deny that I feel the same way about him.

BOB: Is that why Vermeer painted the **blue chair** between the two of you? To suggest that there is some sort of barrier for your love to overcome?

TUTOR: You are very perceptive. Master Vermeer never painted anything without a reason. Everything in our painting has its place.

BOB: Speaking of things in their places, the **mirror** above the lady's head reveals something interesting. Seen from the back, the lady seems to be looking down at her hands on the keyboard. But in the mirror, Vermeer has painted her looking at you.

TUTOR: It is a rather creative clue to the nature of our relationship.

BOB: Vermeer seems to be saying that the young lady is too shy to return your gaze in real life. So he uses the mirror to reveal her true desire.

STUDENT: I must admit, he captured my thoughts in a unique way.

TUTOR: Since you're looking in the mirror, do you see what else Master Vermeer included there?

BOB: I can see what looks like an **easel**, right above the lady's head. Is that Vermeer's easel?

TUTOR: It is, indeed.

BOB: But why would he allow us to see his easel?

TUTOR: I've had many years to think about this, and here's my theory: Vermeer loved giving life to paint. I saw that with my own eyes. And he knew that his paintings would live on long after he died. So in this painting, he included a hint of himself in the form of his easel.

BOB: In other words, just as it did with the young lady, the mirror reveals Vermeer's true desire, which was to live on in his paintings.

TUTOR: Precisely.

BOB: I like how you think. So there are actually two love stories going on here. The one between you and the lady and the one between Vermeer and painting.

TUTOR: I think that sums it up quite nicely.

Sheet music (ca. 1600–1700)

Bibliography

Bailey, Anthony. *Vermeer: A View of Delft*. New York: Henry Holt, 2001.

Chevalier, Tracy. *Girl with a Pearl Earring*. New York: Dutton, 2000.

Duparc, Frederik J., and Arthur K. Wheelock, Jr. *Johannes Vermeer*. Washington, DC: National Gallery of Art; The Hauge: Royal Cabinet of Paintings Mauritshuis; New Haven, CT: Yale University Press, 1995.

Gowing, Lawrence. *Vermeer*. London: Faber and Faber, 1952.

Janson, Jonathan. *Essential Vermeer*. April 19, 2008. http://www.essentialvermeer.com (August 14, 2008).

Montias, John Michael. *Vermeer and His Milieu*. Princeton, NJ: Princeton University Press, 1989.

Snow, Edward A. *A Study of Vermeer*. Berkeley: University of California Press, 1979.

Steadman, Philip. *Vermeer's Camera: Uncovering the Truth behind the Masterpieces*. New York: Oxford University Press, 2001.

Vreeland, Susan. *Girl in Hyacinth Blue*. Denver: MacMurray & Beck, 1999.

Wheelock, Arthur K. *Vermeer: The Complete Works*. New York: Harry N. Abrams, 1997.